Workbook Three Of the Business Essentials Series

LEVERAGING YOUR BUSINESS HARDER

John Millar

Copyright © 2016 John Millar

All rights reserved. No part of this publication may be reproduced, distributed, or transmitted in any form or by any means, including photocopying, recording, or other electronic or mechanical methods, without the prior written permission of the publisher, except in the case of brief quotations embodied in critical reviews and certain other noncommercial uses permitted by copyright law

All rights reserved.

ISBN: 1534941436
ISBN-13: 9781534941434

DEDICATION

I dedicate this book to my mother and father, who raised me while self-employed. They taught me to work hard and listen to everyone but to make my own choices as to what is right and what is wrong.. and oh, did I mention work hard?

Anyone who tells you to work smart not hard hasn't ever done it tough and realized that if you work smart AND hard you will achieve more than you can possibly dream.

CONTENTS

	Dedication	i
1	Product Description	Pg 1
2	Workbook Content	Pg 2
3	7 Steps to More Profit in Less Time	Pg 8
4	The Business Essentials Series	Pg 19
5	About the Author	Pg 22
6	Client Testimonial	Pg 23

PRODUCT DESCRIPTION

LEVERAGING YOUR BUSINESS HARDER

In this important and informative DVD, you'll discover the importance of these questions and how they apply to your business:

- What is leverage?
- Why does your business need it?
- What are the basic principles of leverage?
- What are the benefits of leverage?
- Does it apply to my business?
- What tests and measures can I apply to get the cutting-edge advantage?
- How can I work smarter and not harder?
- How can I reclaim time from a busy schedule?

This is the nitty-gritty of moving from hard work to much-earned success. This is where businesses begin to actually enjoy their success and bask in the glow of their newly acquired knowledge. Many business owners foolishly think they already have the answers and ignore this essential opportunity to access the living, changing, innovative elements that could mean the difference between success and devastating failure. Being in control is the best news you can receive about your business. The information contained in this DVD is the life-blood of any successful business. If you don't have it – you're not surviving. And you're definitely not thriving.

Join the growing number of motivated business owners who have taken advantage of the important training.

Your business can't afford to stay still.

Regards,
John Millar

Leverage is all about getting more with less inside your business, dividing to multiply.

....

....

....

In most of our experience we find that a lot of people actually just bought themselves a job, and as we've said before job really just stands for Just Over Broke.

Just Over Broke

....

....

....

....

I want you to start to think about your business in a completely different way, when you think about things is not a job, your mind expands and amazingly you see your business as an organic thing that you can actually help grow.

We look at a business like a milking stool with three legs:

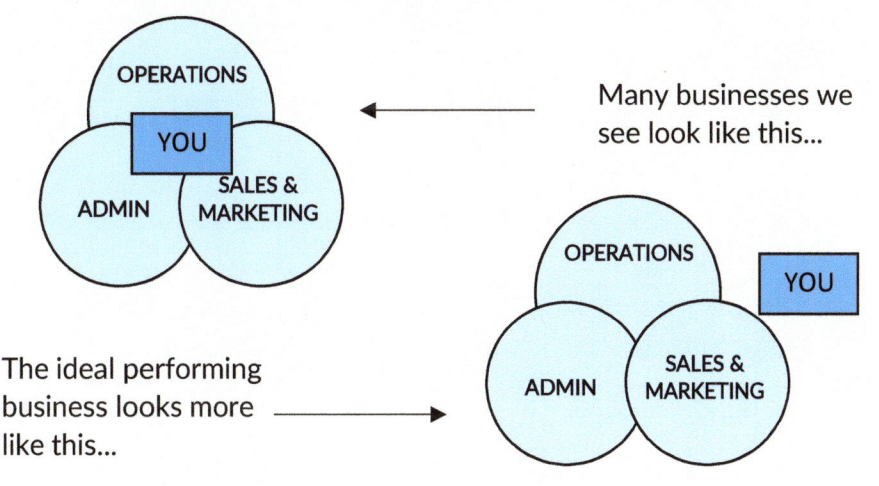

Many businesses we see look like this...

The legs must have same width and the same length otherwise it becomes imbalanced

The ideal performing business looks more like this...

LEVERAGING YOUR BUSINESS HARDER

> If you're not doing those things right, then how can you actually make sure that you can serve your customers with that fantastic product and service that I'm sure that you provide?

As an employee we learn and earn and unfortunately that's where many business owners mindset stops

_____
_____
_____
_____

> Part of the problem is most business owners I first meet put themselves on a wage just like they had when they were an employee instead of focusing on retained earnings within their business

When you become self-employed, you are now stuck having to both get the work and do the work, the treadmill has started!

_____
_____
_____
_____

After we have taken on staff we now required to call ourselves as mangers where we've now taken the business into whole different level and scope where most people just don't have any real experience.

_____
_____
_____
_____
_____

> Eventually as you graduate from earning money to managing people and assets, we now no longer just need to just be good at what we do, but really great of about how we do it!

_____
_____

LEVERAGING YOUR BUSINESS HARDER

This is when we move on to where we move from being a manager and to where we actually being an owner of that business.

Earlier we talked about the cycle of business, where the business owner looks after the team, the team looks after the customer, the customer looks after the business and the business is looking after the business owner?

We quite often see business owners who so heavily involved in their business that they're not really managing their business at all and they most certainly not acting is an owner in their business!

PLEASE talk to your financial adviser and accountant and other wealth advisors, who can actually give you the advice you need to build a business and strategic plan that gives you the best possible leverage.

Businesses are rarely designed to make you wealthy but they can help you make the money to invest in other wealth building strategies like stocks and shares, other businesses, property and so on. Just remember you can't be an expert in all of them just find one that works with you, get the right advice and stay focused!

JOHN MILLAR

> Richard Branson to me is a wonderful example of an entrepreneur, he creates money with other people's ideas and networks as well as his own businesses.

Take a few minutes at the moment and take a note yourself in notebook to think about what level in your business that you currently at and what is your goal?

> Not everybody's goal it to become an entrepreneur, some people just want to become really good self-employed people and that's okay, that's your goal

There are four areas to leverage inside a business.

Leverage through people.

Leverage through systems.

Leverage through marketing.

Leverage through finance.

```
                    Business Strategy
                    ↓      ↓  ↑       ↑
            EBITDA    Working    Inventory
                      Capital
               ↓       ↓  ↑       ↑
                    Free Cash Flow
                ↓   ↑           ↓   ↑
              Equity          Borrowed Capital
                    Capital Structure
```

The very first Porsche was built was built on the chassis of a VW. Now, that's leverage!

Secrets don't have to remain as secrets, they just stay a secret until people either take the time to work it out themselves or haven't yet exposed to the answer yet. – John Millar

Let's put some of the numbers back into your business

LEVERAGING YOUR BUSINESS HARDER

If you increase each of the individual areas within the 7 steps to more profit in less time by just 10% you will have massive compound increases in your business!

7 Steps to More Profit Less Time

Area	Current Figure	Areas of Potential	Increase	New Forecast
Number of Enquiries	4,000	Host Beneficiary, Strategic Alliance, Website SEO, Networking Groups	10%	4,400
Conversion %	25%	Defined USP, Quality Guarantee, Sales Training, CRM	10%	27.5%
	1,000			1,210
Retained Customers	2,000	Members Kit, Newsletters, Customer Surveys, Loyalty Program	10%	2,200
	3,000			3,410
Average $ Sale	$100	Increase Prices, Use a checklist, Offer Finance, Upsell and Cross Sell	10%	$110
Average of Transaction	2	Have an engaged database, Sell more consumables, Build a relationship	10%	2.2
	$600,000			$825,220
Average GP Margin %	25%	NO DISCOUNTING, Reduce Waste, Negotiate better trading terms, Measure everything	10%	27.5%
	$150,000			$266,935.20
Fixed Costs	25%	Better time management, Systemize the routine, Reduce Duplication	10%	$90,000
	$150,000			$136,935.50

LEVERAGING YOUR BUSINESS HARDER

What are ten things that you can do to improve the numbers of new and referral enquiries you get?

1. ....
2. ....
3. ....
4. ....
5. ....
6. ....
7. ....
8. ....
9. ....
10. ....

What are ten things that you can do to improve your conversion rate?

1. ....
2. ....
3. ....
4. ....
5. ....
6. ....
7. ....
8. ....
9. ....
10. ....

What are ten things that you can do to improve your client retention?

1. ....
2. ....
3. ....
4. ....

5. ....
6. ....
7. ....
8. ....
9. ....
10. ....

What are ten things that you can do to increase your average dollar sale?

1. ....
2. ....
3. ....
4. ....
5. ....
6. ....
7. ....
8. ....
9. ....
10. ....

What are ten things that you can do to improve the number of transactions you can do with your clients each month / quarter / year etc?

1. ....
2. ....
3. ....
4. ....
5. ....
6. ....
7. ....
8. ....
9. ....

LEVERAGING YOUR BUSINESS HARDER

10. _____

What are ten things that you can do to improve the gross profit margin with all of your products and services?

1. _____
2. _____
3. _____
4. _____
5. _____
6. _____
7. _____
8. _____
9. _____
10. _____

What are ten things that you can do to decrease your fixed costs?

1. _____
2. _____
3. _____
4. _____
5. _____
6. _____
7. _____
8. _____
9. _____
10. _____

All of your strategies must be tested and measured by key performance indicators.

KPIs these areas and standards by which we are willing judge our business as to how well it's actually performing and whether or not we are going to achieve our goals.

So, what's your business actually all about, what is your business fundamental?

....

....

....

....

....

....

....

Have you worked through your business numbers using the 7 steps formula?

....

....

....

....

So what's holding your business back from increasing your profits?

1. ....
2. ....
3. ....
4. ....
5. ....
6. ....
7. ....
8. ....
9. ....
10. ....

LEVERAGING YOUR BUSINESS HARDER

> Remember when we were setting a goal over the next 12 months we need to actually set a goal with an end in mind.

SMART goals are specific, measurable, achievable, results-driven and realistic and also have a really specific timeframe around it.

WARNING

Goals may cause systematic problems in organisations due to narrowed focus, unethical behaviour, increased risk taking, decreased cooperation, and decreased intrinsic motivation.

Use care when applying goals in your organisation.

What are the 10 strategies that you can implement in your business, in the next 90 days, which will increase over the next 12 months, the profitability of your business?

1.
2.
3.
4.
5.
6.
7.
8.
9.
10.

> Information without application is an obscenity.
> John Millar

> The more your understand where your business has been, where it is today and where you want to take it, the more you comprehend the reality of your business and develop a brightness of the future and make more intelligent

LEVERAGING YOUR BUSINESS HARDER

Develop a strategic plan and make sure you incorporate it your business plan

Get really clear what you are going to do in the next 90 days to achieve those goals and put it all into your 90 day plan

------

You are going to need to allocate time in your default diary throughout the day and throughout the week to make sure you give yourself the zone time to actually work on and in your business.

Go through your action and activity list and choose which of those 5 strategies you need to get a start on NOW to get movement and momentum in each of the 7 steps

------

You don't have to get them finished, you don't have to get them started. Remember you're probably going to going to make a lot of mistakes along the way just don't forget we learn from our mistakes.

LEVERAGING YOUR BUSINESS HARDER

Test and measure to the very best of your ability, every aspect and activity in your business and the results you achieve.

....
....
....
....
....

Make sure that you have constructed and deconstructed your business in a way that it actually makes sense to you and encourages you to drive your business forward.

....
....
....
....
....

What are the top-ten things in my business that you really want and need to measure?

1. ....
2. ....
3. ....
4. ....
5. ....
6. ....
7. ....
8. ....
9. ....
10. ....

How can you begin to measure your success?

1.
2.
3.
4.
5.
6.
7.
8.
9.
10.

> Get and work your numbers for once you truly understand the what, how and why of your numbers you're going to achieve great things.

My name is John Millar, I am the managing director of more profit less time and I am very grateful for the opportunity that i have had to spend with you today to Go through how to leverage your business better. I know that if look at leveraging When and where you can that it will allow you to generate more profit in less time.

Keep this page blank for photocopying

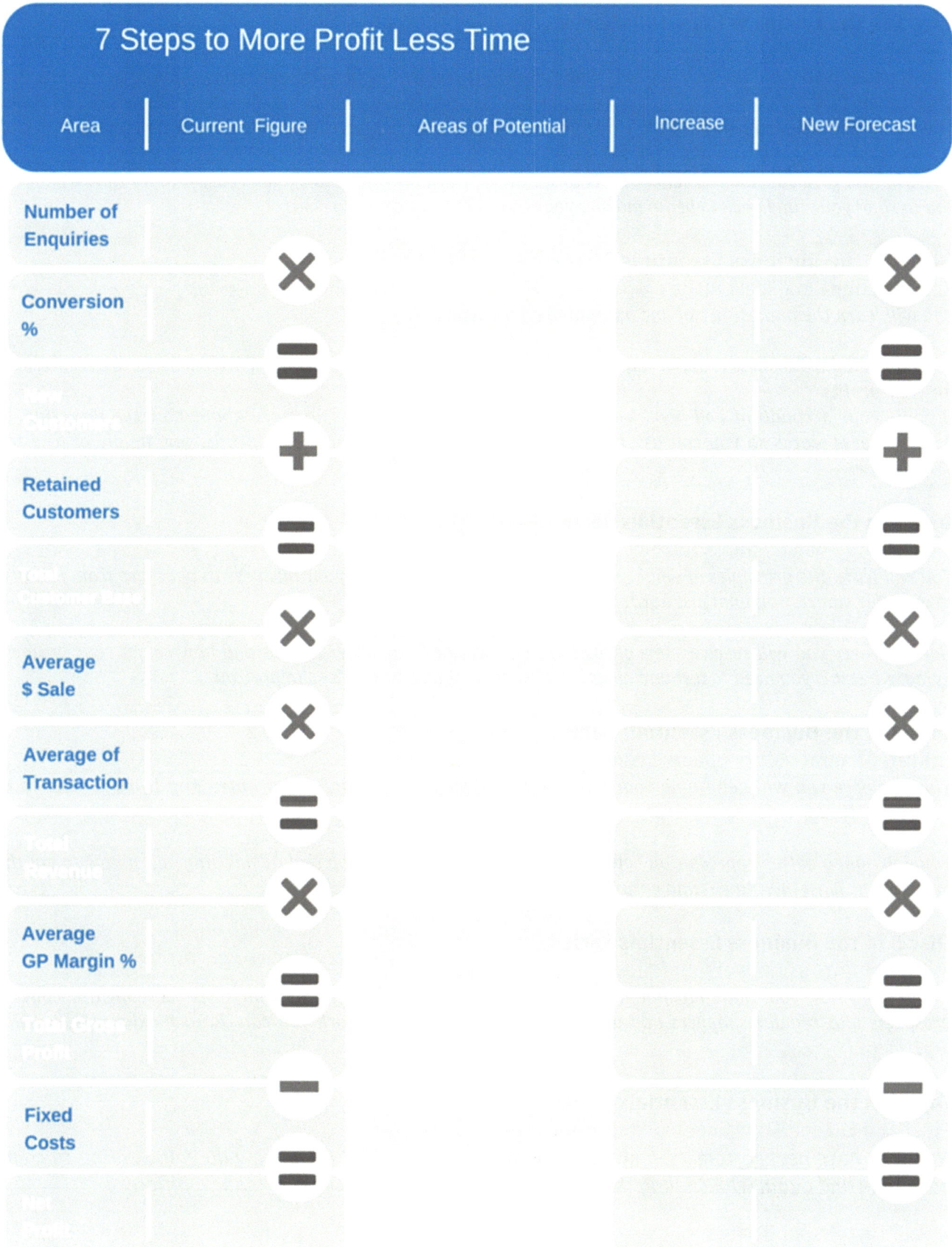

Business Essentials Series...

Disc 1 in the Business Essentials Series
Gaining Focus in Your Business

This is about your fundamental learning skills and what you will need to do to change them to vastly improve the way you look
at your development to become a truly effective business owner not just simply remain self-employed.

You will also give you some excellent tools to set goals, work on your plans and create a diary that will allow you to steal your time back to begin moving your business from chaos to control.

Disc 2 in the Business Essentials Series
Getting Your Financials Right

You will learn the importance of understanding your financials.

After all being in business is about making profit and having cash flow work for YOU since you are responsible for your profits.
Become your accountant and book keepers best friend by understanding more about how the financials in your business works so you can ask them better questions to maximise your profits not simply ensure tax compliance.

Disc 3 in the Business Essentials Series
Leveraging Your Business Harder

You will learn the principles of what and how to leverage far more in your business to get more from less and to work far smarter and not just harder.

Here is where you will receive some of the tools you will need to better understand how to get your business flying, what it is you need to test and measure, how to do it and WHY it's so important.

Disc 4 in the Business Essentials Series
How to Generate More Clients Profitably

This is where you will determine your uniqueness, develop a meaningful guarantee and learn the basics of good advertising.

You will gain a better appreciation between the difference of Marketing and Advertising, learn how to get the most for the least investment and ensure that you do it all profitably.

Disc 5 in the Business Essentials Series
Maximising Your Conversion Rates

Get to know how your Sales Pipeline REALLY works and how to identify who your suspects really are, convert prospects into regular shoppers and understand how much more work you can do to maximise your sales experience.

Disc 6 in the Business Essentials Series
Meet and Exceed Your Clients Expectations

Now you have new customers, how do you make sure you KEEP them, how do you wanting to come back time and again while telling their friends? ...this is where you really make a difference.

Disc 7 in the Business Essentials Series
Systemising Your Business For Consistent Excellence
Do you recognise the importance of having systems in your business and how they can improve your profitability?

We show you how to systemise like a corporate while retaining the culture of a smaller business. Understanding how we systemise for routine and humanise for the exceptions will enable you to be the best in your field every time.

Disc 8 in the Business Essentials Series
Do You Have a Champion Team with a Champion Leader?
This is about having the right people on the bus. It starts with you however so you'll learn how to maximise your own skills and then you will attract and retain the right people.

When you understand how the TEAM is the most important part of your business and what needs to be done to achieve the very best from yourselves and others you are well on your way to becoming a better manager of this invaluable resource.

Disc 9 in the Business Essentials Series
The Essentials of Getting Your Time Back.
This is where you get to redefine your time management You will understand better how you can start working far more on the business than in the business than ever before.

You will also finally find out why others can seem to fit more into their day while having a great LIFE – WORK balance (notice the order!)..

Disc 10 in the Business Essentials Series
Simply Brilliant Customer Service.
It's so easy to give mediocre or good customer service but it's just as easy to give amazing service to your customers and delight them.

You will understand the simple easy steps that you must take to provide consistently brilliant service and how to get your team excited about doing it.

Disc 11 in the Business Essentials Series
Discovering DISC and EQ not just IQ.
We believe for things to change first you must change so here you will learn why you behave as you do and just as importantly understand why other people react and act the way they do.

You will also learn what DISC really is and what it isn't. You will learn how to apply these important principles in your recruitment and team management / development.

You will learn how to use these ideas in creating a more dynamic team and discover the what and why of emotional intelligence. You will also develop key strategies for using the knowledge here and the tools we have available on our website and why we place such a massive emphasis on DISC and other tools that support, train and develop your team.

You will also learn how to use these skills and observations at home and socially not just at the workplace.

Disc 12 in the Business Essentials Series
Quality Recruitment.

Recruitment of the right people for the right reasons in the right roles for your team is so incredibly important yet so often ignored or pushed to the rear.

You will learn who the right person is for your business and the role you want filled.
You will be able to identify the right people early in the process to save yourself and them the time and money wasted with antique recruitment methodologies that just don't work anymore.

How to get the best out of your recruitment activities so you can keep the assets you acquire for the long term and get the best return from your investment.

ABOUT THE AUTHOR

John Millar is the Managing Director, Senior Business Coach Trainer and Consultant with More Profit Less Time Pty Ltd and CEO-ONDEMAND. Along with his many other business interests, John is proud to have been an associate of the most successful coaching team in the world.

He is recognized as a global leader and has been benchmarked against over 1,300 colleagues in 31 countries. John has over 25 years of hands-on ownership, management, coaching, and entrepreneurial experience in a broad range of industry sectors, including retail, wholesale, import, export, IT, trades and trade services, automotive, primary production, food services, transport, manufacturing, mining, professional services, the fitness industry, and more.

He has extensive experience developing and providing training for small to medium-sized companies and a variety of publicly listed corporate companies. John is an accomplished and talented public and professional speaker. He has been a mentor working with sales/management activities for businesses with a turnover under $100,000 per annum, over $100 million turnover, and everything in between, with great success.

John currently works with business owners and their teams across Australia and has a "Whatever it takes" attitude that has enabled him to help his clients grow their business profits by up to 800%.

If you are ready to be coached by one of the best in the business, register at:

www.ceo-ondemand.com.au

Make sure to visit www.moreprofitlesstime.com for the new online Management Development Program: The Business Essentials Series.

ACCLAIM FOR JOHN MILLAR'S
Business Coaching and Training in their own words…

"Without John Millar as my Business Coach I wouldn't have a business today."—Grant Jennings Managing Director, Jigsaw Projects

"Taking the decision to be coached and trained by John Millar was carefully considered after experiencing those who over promised and under delivered. I am pleased to say the content of his courses are the tools we all need to master as business owners. His delivery is engaging, thought provoking and empowering and after every session l came away re-energised. John always makes himself available for business building advice both via Skype and face to face beyond the scope of delivery. With his extensive personal experience in building small businesses, he knows and understands what it takes to establish and grow a business. I have no hesitation endorsing John Millar as an educator and business coach and the bonus is he is a very nice person."—Anne Lederman Managing Director FB Salons"

Johns training with my management team was excellent, it was very different from the business coaching and support I have had in the past. John was clear, thoughtful and he addressed the issues we needed to cover without us even knowing they were being addressed! His follow up has been fantastic and exactly what I needed. I would recommend John and his team to anyone looking at getting some business coaching and training done" —Wendy Crawford, Peopleworx

"In my dealings with John as our business coach, I have found him to be a motivated and insightful agent of positive change. He is able to burrow down to the root cause of issues and introduce effective forms of measurement. John then identifies and implements practical solutions and is there to provide the gentle persuasion required to ensure that results are achieved." —Mark Felton, Lindale Insurances

"You have coached and trained us so well throughout the year that we are now used to & find it easy to prepare a 90 day plan, then breaks it down to actionable bite size pieces. Planning in business & personal life certainly is important. It allows us to identify the important things & the bigger picture. Thank you for your support & guidance throughout the year. And not to mention your insight, external perspective to review & assist our business moving forward." —Linda Turner, Director Roy A McDonald Certified Practicing Accountants

"If you want to achieve sales results you never thought were possible and give yourself a competitive edge my strong suggestion is to engage John services and listen closely to what John has to say, during the time I was trained by John I was one of eight sales consultants in a national business for 10 out of the 13 months I lead the sales tally and in 1 quarter I generated three times the revenue of the national sales force combined. Johns training and experience was well worth the investment and paid big dividends. Thanks John." —Julian Fadini, Bellvue Capital

"John is a very enthusiastic trainer and business coach, he is very passionate about getting business owners and their team where they need to be. He goes the extra mile to keep ahead of the latest developments which he then uses to benefit his clients." —Darren Reddy CPA

"I have been to a few seminars and heard John speak numerous times about sales, marketing and business. He is a very knowledgeable and extremely enthusiastic business coach in all his interactions and I would recommend him to all business owners who need a sales and marketing boost!" —Andrew Heath, Managing Director, Fresh Living Group

"I worked with John Millar and found his business knowledge, passion and innovation to be inspiring. He has always been able to set (and achieve) strategic long and short-term goals both for himself and his clients without losing that personal connection he builds with everyone he meets. He has been and I believe will continue to be a strong mentor and trainer for anyone wanting to take that next step in their business." —Bree Webster, Online Marketing Guru

"Massive Action Day" – what an understatement, John Millars 4 hour frenzy challenged me to seriously review areas of my business I would not have gone to …. In this way, the process identified incongruence's in my mind, my business and my modus operandi. It's created a paradigm shift. Thanks John, the road map just got a whole lot clearer. Your friendship and insights since 2003 have been a gift to my business and I." —Andrew Reay, Counsellor, Hypnotherapist and Counsellor, Thinkshift Transformations

"John Millar is not your usual Business coach or trainer; he gets involved with you and your business and provides hands on help to make sure you follow through on his advice. He is highly motivated to help his clients and his personal guarantee certainly shows this. He has now transposed his thoughts, advice and love of good business onto a series of DVD's in his business venture – More Profit Less Time. This has excellent tips and advice for anyone either starting out or already in business. I highly recommend John to any business owner who wants to run a business and not a j.o.b.!" —Darren Cassidy, Managing Director HR2U

"I and many of my Business Partners and colleagues have worked with John since 2010 as our business oath, trainer and motivator and found him to be an extremely motivational person to assist us achieve our business goals. This company and its products allows for John's skill set to be accessed by a wider number of potential clients. His very professional DVD series is extremely good value for money and is easily accessible for all of us who are time poor. If you are looking to maximise your and your business's results and to start achieving your goals and dreams, contact John; you won't look back!!" —Mark Cleland, Mortgage Choice

"John develops real relationships with the people he comes into contact with. He is pasionate about what he does. His DVD and group training series, is full of good ideas and process to make your business better. Knowing what to do and actually doing it are two different things. John is excellent at helping you get things done." —Carey Rudd, Sales Director, Online Knowledge

"I have known John since 2004 and found him to be extremely knowledgably in both Sales and Business systems as a business coach without peer. John has provided me with business advice as well as personal coaching over the years, helping me with the running of my organisation. I'm impressed with John's DVD series where he has condensed a lot of the information in an easy to follow format that any business owner can use immediately. I wish he had released these DVDs earlier, as they are a goldmine of information, and practical how to that allow anyone to increase the profit in their business and get back valuable wasted time." —Steve Psaradellis, Managing Director, TEBA

"John's DVD and workbook delivery of his no-nonsense advice provides a low-cost option for those business owners looking to set and achieve goals that will increase profit. I found the conversational style of the DVD's easy to follow, whilst the requirement to pause the DVD and write down some action points ensured a level of commitment to the advice being provided." — Mark Felton, Lindale Insurances

"I only met John briefly at a BNI meeting and knew instantly i need to hire him for my business as my business coach. His attitude towards work and how to improve my cash line had an instant effect on before, even before I finally hired him on an official basis. I found myself thinking "what would John do" and this was only after just meeting him. I cannot see my business expend and give me "More Profit Less Time" without John's expert direction and training. If you want to succeed in business life, you need John Millar, without him you're just kidding yourself " —Leslie Cachia, Managing Director, Letac Drafting

"I can highly recommend John Millar to any business owner who wants to grow his business. When I hear very positive feedback from colleagues who are skeptics by nature about John's ability and skills, I know John will help all those he comes in contact with. John comes with a selfless nature and the willingness to work inside a client's business to make it succeed. Rare indeed!" —Darren Cassidy, Managing Director, HR2U"I first met John Millar in mid-2010 and have always found him to be of an honest and generous character that engenders an easy association with him. I love how easy he is to listen to and how passionate he is about his work and topics. John demonstrates a love for life and his work and I have no hesitation in recommending his services." —Kathie M Thomas, Managing Director, VA

"I have listened to John speak on a number of occasions and find him a very knowledgeable speaker with a passion for what he does. I have also interacted with a number of his clients and they all tell me that he helps them achieve results in their business. If you are looking for business help John is a person you can trust." —Carey Rudd, Sales Director, Online Knowledge

"John knows his stuff, he knows how the get results, John has so many great ideas in building a business and helping business owners work less and make more money. John has released a DVD set on doing just that. I have watched the 1st one and it was great, very informative and easy to understand, I happily recommend John to anyone in need of help and guidance" —Frank Eramo, Proprietor, Dynotune

"I have known John only for a short time, however the impact that he has had on me, not just my business has helped me to visualise opportunities that I began to doubt my ability to realise. He is encouraging and at the same time challenging so that he can/you can, begin to see how to maximise the business potential, John calls it being an unreasonable friend, I call it being a mate. If you have any questions about the direction of your business, if you want to seem your bottom line improve not just turnover but real profit, if you want a person who will work with you then I strongly recommend that you engage him at your earliest convenience. John is the best thing that has happened to my business. I could tell you about the way he is on track to make 1/2 a million for me on his contacts alone, but that actually sells him short, he has become like my partner in business, and cares about my success as if it was his own, we will flourish because I took the step to employ his training to help me grow. If you get a chance to get him training you, don't wait like I did, get in as quickly as possible, his time is your business and if like me your business is to make money, then every day you don't have him on retainer you lose money." —Russell Summers, Managing Director, The Give Life Centre

"It's usually easy to be mediocre in business but it's impossible when you have John Millar training you. He has been my right hand since 2003!" —David Manser, CFO, Hydrosteer

"I now have a commercial, profitable business and now it's my choice when I work IN my business and when I work ON it and have had john helping me in business since 1988. I can't imagine not having John as a part of our business." —David Wall, Director, D&K Transport

"The work John has done since 2008 coaching and training our marketing team, administration and finance teams, buyers, store managers and staff nationally have been fantastic." —Ross Sudano, Director, Anaconda Adventure Stores

"John is a creative, professional, practical and committed business coach and trainer. His approach since we first met him in 1994 to working with a client team through the application of useful tools, information and anecdotes along with his easy going & easy to understand delivery sets him apart from other business coaches that I have used in the past." —Anthony Beasley, Director, The Astra Group

"I have worked with John Millar for the since 2004 and I didn't think it was possible to achieve what we have achieved together. His business coaching, training and services just get better and better!" —Terrance Chong, Managing Director, Echo Graphics and Printing

"John's business coaching, training and support has transformed our business across Australia and New Zealand since 2008."—Rose Vis, Managing Director, VIP Australia

"We first met John in 2005, he is AMAZING at sales, marketing, operations, logistics, finance training and so much more. Since engaging John as our business coach our business has exploded, our team are happy, our clients are raving about us and my husband and I now take at least 12 weeks holidays a year, EVERY year." —Shirley Du, Director, Goldline Technology

"It's the no nonsense results driven business coaching and training focus John bought to the table that had such a massive effect on our business." —David Runkel, Director, Tracomp Fabrication and Steel

"We started working with John in early 2010, within 90 days of working with and being trained by John Millar we had the biggest and most profitable month in our 15 year history. That's impressive." —Hugh Gilchrist, Managing Director, Australian Moulding Company

"If you don't have John as your business trainer you aren't meeting your business potential." — Don Robertson, Director, Medallion Electrical Services

Thank You!